# Meet the
# Dinosaurs

# Conoce los
# dinosaurios

## FIRST EDITION

**Series Editor** Penny Smith; **Art Editor** Leah Germann; **US Editors** Elizabeth Hester, John Searcy;
**DTP Designer** Almudena Díaz; **Pre-Production Producer** Nadine King; **Producer** Sara Hu;
**Picture Research** Myriam Megharbi; **Dinosaur Consultant** Dougal Dixon;
**Reading Consultant** Linda Gambrell, PhD

## THIS EDITION

**Editorial Management** by Oriel Square
**Produced for DK** by WonderLab Group LLC
Jennifer Emmett, Erica Green, Kate Hale, *Founders*

**Editors** Grace Hill Smith, Libby Romero, Michaela Weglinski; **Spanish Translation** Isabel C. Mendoza;
**Photography Editors** Kelley Miller, Annette Kiesow, Nicole DiMella;
**Managing Editor** Rachel Houghton; **Designers** Project Design Company;
**Researcher** Michelle Harris; **Copy Editor** Lori Merritt; **Indexer** Connie Binder;
**Proofreaders** Carmen Orozco, Larry Shea; **Reading Specialist** Dr. Jennifer Albro;
**Curriculum Specialist** Elaine Larson

**Published in the United States by DK Publishing**
1745 Broadway, 20th Floor, New York, NY 10019

A catalog record for this book
is available from the Library of Congress.
HC ISBN: 978-0-7440-8373-6
PB ISBN: 978-0-7440-8372-9

DK books are available at special discounts when purchased in bulk for sales promotions, premiums,
fundraising, or educational use. For details, contact: DK Publishing Special Markets,
1745 Broadway, 20th Floor, New York, NY 10019
SpecialSales@dk.com

Printed and bound in China

The publisher would like to thank the following for their kind permission to reproduce their images:
a=above; c=center; b=below; l=left; r=right; t=top; b/g=background

**Alamy Images:** W. Wayne Lockwood, MD 4-5cb/g, 8-9b/g, Charles Mauzy 5tclb/g, 24-25 b/g, Craig Tuttle 4brb/g,
14-15b/g, 28-29b/g, 30acr, Phil Wilson/Stocktrek Images 16-17, Larry Lee Photography 18-19b/g, 30acl, Robert Harding
Picture Library Ltd 20-21b/g, 30ac, Jim Zuckerman 30bl; **Corbis:** Matt Brown 26-27b/g; **DK Images:** Jon Hughes 4-5c,
8-9b/g, 8b; **Getty Images:** James Randklev 4cb/g, 10-11b/g, J.P. Nacivet 22-23b/g, 30br;
**Getty Images / iStock:** Orla 6-7b/g, dottedhippo 9b

Cover images: *Front:* **Dorling Kindersley:** Alexandra Bye (volcano), Jenny Wren cl, br;
*Back:* **Dorling Kindersley:** Alexandra Bye tl, Jenny Wren cr, bl

All other images © Dorling Kindersley
For more information see: www.dkimages.com

For the curious
**Para los curiosos**
www.dk.com

# Meet the
# Dinosaurs

# Conoce los
# dinosaurios

**DK**

Look!
Here come
the dinosaurs.

¡Mira!
Aquí vienen
los dinosaurios.

This dinosaur
has sharp teeth.

Este dinosaurio tiene
dientes afilados.

## Tyrannosaurus

[tie-RAN-oh-SORE-us]

# Tiranosaurio

This huge
dinosaur has
a long neck.

Este enorme
dinosaurio tiene
un cuello largo.

## Brachiosaurus

[BRAK-ee-oh-SORE-us]

# Braquiosaurio

This dinosaur has three horns.

Este dinosaurio tiene tres cuernos.

**Triceratops**

[try-SER-uh-tops]

# Triceratops

This fast dinosaur has sharp claws.

Este rápido dinosaurio tiene garras afiladas.

## Velociraptor

[vuh-LOSS-uh-rap-ter]

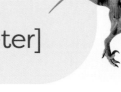

# Velocirráptor

# Corythosaurus

[ko-RITH-oh-SORE-us]

This dinosaur has
a bright crest.

Este dinosaurio tiene una
cresta de colores vivos.

**Coritosaurio**

This dinosaur is small.
It runs fast.

## Compsognathus

[KOMP-sug-NAY-thus]

Este dinosaurio es pequeño.
Corre rápido.

**Compsognathus**

This dinosaur is smart.
It has large eyes.

Este dinosaurio es inteligente.
Tiene los ojos grandes.

**Troodon**

[TROH-oh-don]

# Troodonte

This dinosaur has plates and spikes. It has a tiny brain.

Este dinosaurio tiene placas y espinas. Tiene un cerebro diminuto.

**Stegosaurus**

[STEG-oh-SORE-us]

# Estegosaurio

This dinosaur is tall.
It has thin legs
and a toothless beak.

Este dinosaurio es alto.
Tiene patas delgadas
y un pico sin dientes.

**Gallimimus**

[GAL-uh-MY-mus]

# Gallimimus

# Iguanodon

[ig-WAHN-oh-don]

This strong dinosaur has a spike on each thumb.

Este fuerte dinosaurio tiene una espina en cada pulgar.

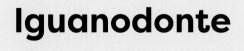

**Iguanodonte**

This dinosaur eats plants. It has a thick skull.

Este dinosaurio come plantas. Tiene un cráneo grueso.

## Stegoceras

[STEG-oh-CER-us]

**Estegoceras**

This tough dinosaur has a tail club.

Este fuerte dinosaurio tiene un garrote en la cola.

**Ankylosaurus**

[an-KAI-loh-SORE-us]

# Anquilosaurio

# Which dinosaur
# do you like best?

## ¿Cuál es el dinosaurio
## que más te gusta?

# Glossary
# Glosario

**Ankylosaurus**
a plant-eating dinosaur with a tail club

**Brachiosaurus**
a very tall plant-eating dinosaur

**Triceratops**
a plant-eating dinosaur with three horns

**Tyrannosaurus**
a large meat-eating dinosaur

**Velociraptor**
a fast, meat-eating dinosaur with sharp claws

**Anquilosaurio**
dinosaurio herbívoro que tiene un garrote en la cola

**Braquiosaurio**
dinosaurio herbívoro muy alto

**Tiranosaurio**
enorme dinosaurio carnívoro

**Triceratops**
dinosaurio herbívoro que tiene tres cuernos

**Velocirráptor**
dinosaurio carnívoro muy rápido que tiene garras afiladas

# Quiz
# Prueba

Answer the questions to see what you have learned.
Check your answers with an adult.

1. Which dinosaur has large eyes?
2. Which dinosaur has plates on its back and spikes on its tail?
3. Which dinosaur has a bright crest on its head?
4. Which dinosaur is small?
5. Imagine if you were a dinosaur for a day. What would you eat? Would you have any special features?

1. Troodon 2. Stegosaurus 3. Corythosaurus 4. Compsognathus
5. Answers will vary

Responde las preguntas para saber cuánto aprendiste.
Verifica tus respuestas con un adulto.

1. ¿Qué dinosaurio tiene los ojos grandes?
2. ¿Qué dinosaurio tiene placas en el lomo y espinas en la cola?
3. ¿Qué dinosaurio tiene una cresta de colores vivos en la cabeza?
4. ¿Qué dinosaurio es pequeño?
5. Imagina que eres un dinosaurio por un día. ¿Qué comerías? ¿Tu cuerpo tendría partes especiales?

1. Troodonte 2. Estegosaurio 3. Coritosaurio 4. Compsognathus
5. Las respuestas pueden variar.